Goulden House Selling Rules

The basics to preparing your home, selling your home, avoiding costly mistakes, and negotiating the sale to get exactly what you want.

The Author has strived to be as accurate and complete as possible in the creation of this report, notwithstanding the fact that he does not warrant or represent at any time that the contents within are accurate due to the rapidly changing nature of the Internet.

While all attempts have been made to verify information provided in this publication, the Author assumes no responsibility for errors, omissions, or contrary interpretation of the subject matter herein. Any perceived slights of specific persons, peoples, or organizations are unintentional.

In practical advice books, like anything else in life, there are no guarantees of income made. Readers are cautioned to rely on their own judgment about their individual circumstances to act accordingly.

This book is not intended for use as a source of legal, business, accounting or financial advice. All readers are advised to seek services of competent professionals in legal, business, accounting, and finance fields.

Table of Contents

It's Not Just a House, It's a Home

In the last 20 years of my marriage, we've bought three homes. Every single time, there was a reason and every single time we had our list of must-haves. But in the end, the top deciding factors were where it was located, how it felt to drive into the neighborhood (and up the driveway), how it would accommodate our family's needs, and what we envisioned for our new life inside this new home.

Purchasing our second home sticks out the most in my mind (okay, in my wife's mind) because when we drove up to that ranch on 2 acres with the detached 4 car garage, I was finished looking.

Even though our realtor had other houses to show us, I told my wife, I didn't need to see any more. My dream was complete with the land and the garage.

I spent many summers tinkering in the garage, waxing my boat and taking care of my truck until they were sparkling clean and shiny. There was one summer that I accidentally ran over a bee's nest with my riding mower, jumped off, screaming and ran into the house with the bees still under my shirt and the mower still running on the lawn. I had never seen bees nest in the ground before, but you better believe, I went and threw fire bombs in the ones I found after that. My wife ended up hanging a brown paper lunch bag on the porch because she read that bees have bad eyesight and would think it was another hive and stay away.

We grew a garden there with raspberries we got from a friend's daughter who owned a farm. I can still taste them now. Those raspberries were so sweet – nothing like the ones that you get in the store. I also planted sunflowers to keep the critters away. And one year, I let our fall pumpkins decompose in the garden and tilled them under only to have a pumpkin patch the next year by accident. The kids still talk about that!

We were raising three kids so the outside space was nice for them to play around. We had a pink and teal Barbie jeep, a Caterpillar backhoe and a police motorcycle power wheel running through the yard frequently. I loved to hear them laugh and play pretend with each other. We ended up finishing the basement so they had more space for their play and toys.

They say, "Home is where the heart is," and I truly believe it. Whenever we've been out of town visiting family or on vacation and we're heading back I think, "It'll be nice to get back home." My wife says she thinks, "I can't wait to be in my own bed."

I really could go on for days about all the great times we had in that ranch. It's memories like these that I want to help other families create, whether you're single or have a large family. I know that buying and selling a home can be a stressful time, especially if it's your first home and I want to change the perception of that. It should be an exciting and happy time where people should look forward and be able to enjoy the process.

See, a house is not just a physical building. It's so much more. It's a home. It's the place where your memories will forever be. The pictures in your mind will be of the inside and outside with the people you care about laughing, playing, being goofy and spending time together.

Because a home is a place where you get to feel comfortable, safe, warm, and cozy. It's the place you can sit around all day in your pjs if you want. You have things around you that are special and have meaning, but most of all you are surrounded by people you love, who love you back.

A family makes a house a home by living in it and making it special. And that's why it's so important to me to help change the perception of home buying and selling as just another transaction. It's where your memories live and you get to take those memories everywhere you go. So it's my mission to make this process as stress free as possible and make it a great experience for you.

Set the Right Expectations - How Long Will It Take to Sell Your Home?

Last year (2019), the average time it took to sell a home was 68 days.

When we sold our ranch home in 2012, it took quite a long time. One of the reasons was a poor housing market and then we had 2 more things going against us: a dirt road, and a property assessment/lien from the township.

The township was moving people on our road to city sewer and for each home on the sewer's road, we had to pay to connect so it wasn't just the township's cost. We had to also hire someone to dig and lay the pipe across our front yard to get to the sewer line. Their requirement was that if we sold our home, the new owners would automatically be required to hook up to the new sewer line upon purchase.

The cost was over $15,000 and for a home that was worth a little over $150,000, adding 10% in owner costs was not attractive.

Luckily for us, the township was not ready for the homeowners on our road to hook up so we got a waiver for this requirement that we passed down to the owners to delay the hookup for a few years. Without that, we might still be in that house.

Here are some of the key factors that impact your selling timeline:

- time of year

- local housing market conditions such as buyer demand and job market

- type of home

- condition of home

- your agent's listing strategy

- other liens/property assessment/loans to pay off

- the amount of time it takes the buyer to secure their loan

Listing your home in the spring seems to generally be the best time of year but that's not true for every home or market. Buyers who are looking for a home during winter or the holidays could have a more urgent reason and be more serious.

Also, if you need to make repairs or updates to your home, that could delay getting your home on the market. It's best to have these items completed before listing if possible so your home shows in the best condition.

Your Goulden Opportunity to Sell Your Home Quickly

Selling your home is where the saying is true that you don't get a second chance to make a first impression – this is your Goulden Opportunity to do it right. The better condition your house is in, the more interest you'll get and it will be evident to the buyer that your asking price is justified.

To make sure that you make a good impression on the prospective buyers, you need to make sure items in your house are in good shape or fixed. As someone living in the house, many things might be normal to you because you have gotten used to them but a buyer will immediately notice.

Any crack in the ceiling or any broken piece of furniture must be fixed before you start showing your house to potential buyers.

My wife notices a lot of things when we go look at houses. It's just her personality to pay a lot of attention to detail and she will notice if the front door is crooked, a porch step is cracked, nails are coming out of drywall, or if a really high end faucet has been installed. On the other hand, she doesn't mind imagining a house without clutter (she admits she an organized mess and I'm told not to move her piles) and I notice when there's a lot of unnecessary items stuffed in the corners.

If you look at things with this kind of eye, you'll find all the things that the buyer may notice too. The main thing you want to convey when someone sees your house is that it's bright, clean, and well-maintained. Most buyers, unless they are investors, will want a house that's as close to move-in condition as possible.

Here's how you can make your house look like it's Goulden:

Declutter

Look at your house from the perspective of someone walking in the front door for the first time. What do you see? Does it feel spacious and inviting? If you can clear countertops, shelves, closets and knick-knacks, your home will look bigger and better maintained. If you need to, consider using a storage unit to keep unnecessary items out of your house while you're showing it.

Decor

Make your home décor as neutral as possible. Tone down colors and crazy wall hangings so that the buyers don't have a strong reaction to something that has nothing to do with the house. Allow the buyers to easily envision their belongings in this space without distraction. You may want to store family photos so they can imagine their own family in this space instead.

Maintenance

If there are any maintenance items that you've put off, now is the time to do them. This includes small and big fixes such as landscaping, wall scuffs, changing your air filter, window, grout, roof, gutters, etc.

Goulden Tips for a Tip Top Showing

You can make your house look amazing starting with a deep cleaning when you list it and then maintaining it while you sell. Less is always more when showing your house so make sure your home is in good working order so you can show off its best features.

The last time we put our house up for sale, we ended up painting the garage door and porch, including repairing a porch spindle. We also wiped down the walls and removed scuffs. The walls that had too much damage, we gave a fresh coat of paint.

INSIDE

- Scrub the whole house including the floors, counters, cabinets, microwave, dishwasher, stovetop, refrigerator and walls. You probably walk by things that you don't notice anymore so try to look at everything with fresh eyes or ask a friend to walk through with you and point things out.

- Paint is one of the best things to do to brighten up a home. It's time well spent.

- Fix creaks, sticky doors, knobs that don't turn well, etc.

- Check your kitchen and bathroom grout for repairs and other stains

- Deep clean rugs and carpets. Replace area rugs if needed or roll them up and store them (area rugs can make a space look smaller). Wash your bathroom floor mats.

- Donate unneeded items or do a garage sale. Get rid of extra clutter, even in your closets because it can make your home seem smaller.

- If you can't declutter, make things look organized.

- Pick up toys and any pet items.

- Store kitchen gadgets and small appliances that you may normally keep out on your counter. Same with your bathroom counter.

- Wash your windows and sills to add extra, clear light

OUTSIDE

- Your porch is one of the first areas a buyer will notice. Make sure it's clean, freshly painted, and repaired if needed. Plants are always a nice touch to make your front door feel welcoming.

- Wash your windows from the outside.

- Take care of any landscaping needs including flowerbeds and weeds. Trim the shrubs.

- Check and clean your gutters

The following is a basic checklist you can refer to when you show your house to prospective buyers.

	Declutter and Store Away Unnecessary Items
	Make Beds
	Clean and clear out closets, empty hampers
	Let there be light – turn on lights, open drapes
	Clean the yard (especially if you have pets)
	Do a sniff test (but don't cover up odors which can make it worse)
	Close the Toilet Lids
	Dust so everything looks sparkly clean
	Vacuum floors
	Clear all countertops
	Clean and shine sink and appliances
	Sweep kitchen floors
	Empty trash
	Lock up valuables
	Set the scene (lay pillows and blanket on couches and bed, set up bathroom like a hotel)

7 Goulden Home Improvements with the Highest Return on Investment

When upgrading and updating your home to sell, keep things neutral and don't go overboard with any project. Pick what appeals to the most people and don't go for the unique, quirky or outlandish fixtures.

1. Kitchen

Some say that kitchens and baths sell a home. Statistics show that you can get back as much as 60% to 120% when investing in a kitchen remodel so long as you don't go overboard. Don't make your kitchen fancier than the rest of the house or the other kitchens in your neighborhood. Keep potential buyers in mind – most people won't pay for a fancy, overdone kitchen with an industrial stove or imported Tuscan tiles.

2. Bathroom

Adding a bathroom, especially if you have only one, is an investment that many can recoup. You can get back 80% or more of your investment. Again, stay on par with your neighborhood.

3. Energy-Efficient Windows

Drafty windows indicate a big cost to potential buyers. They look for energy efficient windows to save money. You could get a green energy tax credit for your new windows too.

4. Building a Deck

Outdoor spaces are really desirable for potential buyers. If you can make your backyard and deck more appealing, your house will look better and could be the deciding factor if your home is competing with another that is similar. If you're handy, you can save money by putting the deck in yourself.

5. Basic Updates

There are some really simple improvements that can have a big impact on how your house presents. Keep the paint fresh, check the plumbing, electrical wiring, fix the roof when it leaks, replace rotted wood, broken spindles, and make sure there is no mold to be found. Buyers will look for signs of routine maintenance as an indication of things they can't see.

6. Garage Door Replacement

On average, replacing your garage door gets you almost a 100% recoupment of your cost nationwide.

7. Steel Entry Door Replacement

It may come as a surprise, but replacing your front door with a steel entry door could get you over 90% of your replacement cost back.

7 Home Improvement Projects to Avoid

Not all home improvement projects will be a Goulden opportunity and value to your home. Some are purely because you like it or it makes your life more comfortable. Don't expect to get that investment back.

Some low-value home improvement projects include:

1. In-Ground Swimming Pools

While some people love pools, others do not and a pool can make your house harder to sell. Many families with small children don't want a pool, so you're eliminating a large number of families. Pools also increase energy cost, requires extra maintenance, and raises your homeowner's insurance.

4. Sunrooms

While this sounds great, especially in Michigan where I live, sunrooms are unfortunately an expensive project with less than 50% investment return. Sunrooms can also raise energy costs in the cold and hot seasons.

5. Professional or Expensive Landscaping

While it would be great to drive up to a beautiful paradise after work, professional or expensive landscaping is only for your enjoyment. Instead of investing here, add curb appeal to your house with a well-kept lawn, low maintenance shrubs or small trees.

6. Full Roof Replacement

While a brand new roof is great for your listing, it's not something that you can add to your listing price. A roof is something that a potential buyer expects you to maintain so they won't pay more for what's necessary. On the flip side, an old or leaky roof will turn off buyers so if it has to be done, it has to be done. Just don't expect to recoup the full cost.

7. Larger Master Suite

If you're using another bedroom to create more room in your master suite, going down from three to two bedrooms could mean a big drop in your selling price. And if you use closet space to add to your master suite, the buyer may not see that room as a bedroom anymore without a closet.

Note: Invisible Home Improvements Maintenance Items

Buyers aren't going to pay extra for maintenance items around your house because they expect the home to be maintained well. If you need to spend money to replace your furnace, air conditioner, hot water unit or septic system, etc., you won't recoup the cost. On the other hand, if any of these aren't working, the buyer may automatically reject your home. These items will show up in your home inspection too, so you'll want to make sure they work.

Top Selling Mistakes

Selling your house can be stressful, but you can look forward to your new home and the new memories waiting for you there. With so many people coming through your house, it may feel hard to juggle all the opinions and feedback that you're getting. Remember that it's exactly that – opinions and feedback.

Take to heart what you need to and leave the rest. Some feedback is just to set up a lower than desired offer. Some feedback is personal preference and some opinions are just not applicable.

You are not required to take action on any of it, but if it is a good suggestion, leave your emotions out of it. Selling your home is very much a business transaction and nothing to take personally.

Here are the top mistakes sellers have when selling their home:

Unrealistic Price Expectations

Setting the right asking price is key to getting your house sold as quickly as possible. Get a comparable analysis report from your agent. Regardless of what you think your house is worth, the price should be based on what similar homes sold most recently.

Remember, it's rare that you'll get what you're asking for. Most buyers will start negotiating lower than what you're asking just to start the conversation.

Overpriced homes don't generally sell well.

Underpriced homes can sometimes create a bidding war, increasing the price to the home's correct market value.

Poor Photo Quality

I'm sure you've seen them – dark photos of rooms taken from a cell phone that makes rooms look very tiny and drab.

Because so many people look for houses online these days, your photos are your home's first impression. Many listings have poor photos with bad lighting so if you have great, bright pictures, your home will stand out even more (and look well taken care of).

Photos should be crisp and clear with plenty of natural light. They should highlight your home's best qualities and attributes. If you can use a wide angle lens, your home will look even more spacious. If you're hiring a real estate agent, ask before you list if the realtor will have wide angle lens photos professionally taken.

Trying to Hide Problems

It's not a great idea to try to save money by hiding a problem, skimping on a fix or duct taping something together. Any problems will be revealed during the inspection so you can either fix the problem or price the property to account for the buyers needing to fix it and disclose the issue. You can also offer the buyer a credit to fix the issue and price your home as if it was fixed.

Just know that not fixing the problem may eliminate some buyers who don't want to bother fixing anything.

One of the projects we hadn't gotten to when we listed our home was replacing our basement ceiling. We had come home from vacation once to find that the ceiling was soft where there had been a leak from above. To avoid any mold or other issues, I cut out the ceiling and we were able to fix the plumbing leak.

Since that bathroom isn't heavily used, it wasn't a top priority. Three years later, the hole was still in that ceiling and we were putting the house on the market. So we had to decide: do we delay putting the house up (we had already found a house we wanted), do we hope they don't notice (not likely), or do we disclose it and make sure it's done before the closing?

We chose to put the house up immediately and I got drywall the next week and put it up. In our listing, we stated that the ceiling in the bathroom would be complete before closing.

Presenting Poorly

Buyers understand that you live in your house, but it has to look well-kept and clean. You don't need to hire a professional stager but it's important to spruce up the inside and outside of your home so that little things don't deter a buyer. If someone thinks that a house hasn't been maintained well, they'll wonder what hidden (and costly) problems may be down the road.

Something as minor as cobwebs or marks on the walls can create a negative experience for some buyers. Invite your agent to point out all areas of your home that could easily be improved. Declutter your closets. Make sure there are no weird smells, especially pets. Fresh paint doesn't cost a lot and can make a huge difference in appeal.

Saying No to Showings

Yes, showings can be requested at inopportune times. It's all temporary. Yes, you need to clean and tidy up (they'll be looking at your closets too). Get your whole family to chip in to make it faster and easier.

Forgoing the Agent

I'm sure it comes as no surprise that I would suggest you have an agent. There's quite a lot of paperwork to be done. Doing it yourself can be overwhelming and it's easy to miss something you need to have.

To help you with what is needed, the following list is taken from https://www.nolo.com/legal-encyclopedia/organizing-paperwork-your-home-sale.html

- the original sales contract for your house, with the purchase price

- documents related to title and ownership of your home, including a property survey, certificate of occupancy, certificates of compliance with building and zoning codes, and the like

- mortgage and financing documents

- tax records you may need to provide the buyer, such as real estate, school, and other tax information

- the professional appraisal done when you bought your house and any documented changes to the appraisal since then

- records regarding your homeowners' insurance

- reports of any professional inspections done before putting your house up for sale

- receipts and documentation of improvements you've made to your house, such as adding a new bathroom

- home repair and maintenance records (although maintenance will not figure into your tax basis)

- manuals and warranty information (you may be including major appliances as part of your sale)

- details on different real estate agents you are considering working with

- if you are in a homeowner's association, all related documents

- anything else relevant to your sale (such as a file on the builder if you are selling a newly built home).

If you do decide not to hire an agent, you'll need to do all your research on pricing yourself and I would suggest hiring a real estate lawyer for your paperwork and the finer points of the transaction and escrow.

Most people think that if they sell their home by themselves, they can keep what would've been the agent's commission. On the contrary, most homes have factored in the commission into their listing price, so without the commission, you may be expected to drop your price in comparison to similar homes. If your buyer has an agent, you'll still be expected to pay that agent's fee.

How Much Will It Cost to Sell Your House?

Calculating how much money you'll walk away with isn't as simple as taking off the commission from your sales price. There are other costs and fees you have to pay or that have been negotiated during the sale. And don't forget any repairs you've made or what you put into the house to get it ready for sale.

When we owned 13 acres, we decided to sell two to a neighbor. We didn't use a lawyer, just a title company. But because we weren't used to this type of transaction, we didn't realize that there were certain costs traditionally assigned to the seller. There were definitely some surprises at closing, but we fortunately had a very gracious purchaser who was willing to pay those costs and we walked away with very close to what we expected. It doesn't always work out this way, so make sure you know your costs.

Here is a list of some of the costs you may have:

- **Realtor Commission.** The seller is responsible for the real estate commission and though it can range, it's generally six percent.

- **Staging your home.** Anything you've bought to make your house present well, including a professional stager.

- **Updates, Repairs or Maintenance.** Anything you decided to fix or update. The buyer could also ask for repairs before closing.

- **Contract Negotiations and Mortgage Fees.** The buyer may have asked you to give them a credit, cover part of the closing costs, title insurance or other fees.

The Goulden Asking Price

What's that magic, Goulden asking price to sell your home quickly and for the most profit? Sellers often feel like their home is worth more because the memories in them are priceless. But when a buyer looks at a house, they sometimes see flaws that a seller would often overlook.

Even though you're selling your home can have some real emotions attached to it, finding the right price can't be made from an emotional place. Pricing your home right when it first hits the market can be the difference between a fast offer or having your house listed for many months with people wondering what's wrong with it.

You can try to look up some homes in your area that are similar to yours to see what's been sold recently or you can ask your agent to prepare a comparable report for you. It's important to know that while you can ask for whatever you want, your home has to appraise for the price if the buyers need a loan.

If you have the luxury of time you may try listing it higher, but if you want it to sell quickly, you'll need to be as competitive as possible. Just remember that the longer your house is on the market (even if you delist and relist it), the more skeptical buyers may become.

Live in Michigan? I'm happy to do a complimentary analysis of your home and market. Just email me at mgould@remax.net with your address.

Elisha Garvock Jakubowski 🔲 recommends Michael Gould Real Estate.
March 18 at 3:57 PM · 🌐

Working with Michael for many years, I can tell you he is one of the most honest and caring persons I know. If you are looking for a realtor that will work hard and have your best interest at heart, this is the man for you.

🔘 Michael Gould Real Estate

Greg Baker 🔲 recommends Michael Gould Real Estate.
March 23 at 11:39 PM · 🌐

I worked with Michael for many years and so highly recommend him. He's smart, genuine and keeps his word. You won't find a better professional.

7 Goulden Negotiation Tips to Help You WIN

To tip the scales in your favor to get your best selling price, you need to set everything up right prior to getting your offer. The perfect offer is rare. You most likely will enter into a discussion where both sides could make concessions.

The best thing to do is to create a listing and a price where the buyer has little to point to that would justify a low offer.

When we bought the home we're currently in, it had been in foreclosure for some time. The landscaping was overgrown, though you could tell that someone had loved landscaping there at some point. However when we got inside, the whole house had been freshly painted and new carpet was throughout. We knew for this house, since we were dealing with the bank, there was little negotiation room.

This wasn't the only house we considered. We also had liked a home that had a little more space, but the interior needed a lot more work. There was ugly wallpaper that needed to be taken down, the master bath had mauve fixtures and the carpet needed to be replaced, along with an old oven.

While we would've been able to negotiate more with the second offer, we decided to go with the foreclosed home because it was move-in ready. I decided that I was more willing to tackle the landscaping versus the interior of the other house (little did I know it would take five summers to finally get looking like I wanted).

As a seller, here are some things to consider when you get the offer:

- Buyer pre-approval

- Closing costs

- Seller concessions

- Cash vs. financing

- Buyer's contingency

- Timeline

Here are seven negotiation tips that can help you win:

1. Prioritize What Matters Most to You

When you list your house (before you get your first offer) write a list of priorities. Is the closing time most important? Is it the price? Is it getting a cash deal?

Know your net profit after all costs and know what your bottom dollar amount is. If price is imperative, you have to be willing to walk from the negotiations. If time is most important, you may need to be more flexible on price.

If you start negotiations without knowing where you stand, you'll automatically feel like you're losing.

2. Know what leverage you have

It's important to know what your competition is and how much competition is out there. The more available inventory, the more risk that your buyer could walk and make an offer on a different house. Know if it's a buyer's market or seller's market and if you are in a seller's market, you know you have more leverage in your negotiations.

3. Price your house right from the beginning

It's important that the price you set when your listing hits the market is attractive to the market. If you overprice your home at the start, you lose leverage while your house stays on the market. Buyers start to wonder what's wrong with the home or if there are hidden problems, even if you lower the price.

4. Reduce Potential Buyer Objections

Avoid requests for credits and fixes by keeping your house well maintained and fixed prior to listing. Anything that is found in the home inspection could land you back into negotiations.

5. Require an earnest money deposit.

Require a deposit when someone makes an offer to show how serious they are. You can ask for a high earnest money deposit, but that doesn't mean that a seller will give you it. Typically, the earnest money deposit ranges between one and three percent.

6. Be Smart When Negotiating Closing Costs

Closing costs are split up between the buyer and the seller. Certain fees have historically been the seller's. These include:

- Both sides of the realtor commissions

- Loan payoff

- Transfer taxes and recording fees

- Title insurance

- Unpaid HOA dues or fees

The buyer's closing costs usually include:

- Mortgage application, origination and underwriting fees

- Prepaid interest

- Appraisal cost

- Home inspection fee

- Pest inspection fee

- Credit report fee

- Title search

- Lender's title insurance

Most of the buyer's fees are associated with their mortgage. But they can ask for the seller to cover some of the costs through the negotiations. Some fees that buyers ask frequently are pest inspection, title search, and home warranty.

Remember that anything you concede hits your bottom line. Refer back to your priorities when deciding what you want to counter offer. Then at closing, make sure to check that the fees are being assigned to the right person.

7. Know When to Walk Away

Again, know your priorities. You don't need to accept any offer, but if you want to open up conversation, you have to counter with something that shows you're willing to negotiate. You can counter as much as you want and it's also great to know prior to entering any negotiations when you'll walk away. Create those parameters beforehand so that you can leave your emotions out of it.

If you walk away after you agree on a sale, you could be in legal trouble and the buyers could enforce the "specific performance" remedy and take you to court to force the sale.

If the buyer walks, they'll lose their earnest money deposit. Your house will go back up on the market and if you know something new from the home inspection, you'll legally have to disclose them to every new buyer.

A note on the win-win concept:

You've probably heard it before. You're encouraged to get to a win-win. You win, I win, we all win. My philosophy is the same as Jim Camp, author of "Start with No", who says it's still a losing game and should be re-dubbed the win-lose negotiation. Maybe we like the idea of win-win because it feels better for everyone to think they all won. But in reality, the person who has the least interest in continuing the negotiations is the one who is more powerful in setting the terms.

Growing up, my dad always told me, "If you don't say anything, you can't get in trouble." However, my wife has since explained to me that I can still get in trouble even if I keep my mouth shut. Nonetheless, my dad's teaching carried with me for much of my life.

Unfortunately, it showed up in my negotiations. I didn't want to create a conflict – speaking up in a negotiation felt like getting in trouble. This was also very evident when I bought my first brand new truck back in 1998, a black Dodge Ram 4X4. I simply knew what I wanted and rather than negotiate, I bought at sticker price. In the end I was left paying way more than I should have, plus got suckered into payment protection insurance that had a penalty when I paid the truck off early. I can say that I definitely did not win there.

More recently in July, I was looking for a new truck lease. I knew I had a lot of options -- a lot of dealerships were having sales, so I could set my terms. I can't even tell you how many times I had the salesperson check with the manager before I walked out with my new 2019 Chevy Silverado, cutting their original monthly payment by about 30 percent, getting an extra 3,000 miles per year for free and a bed liner thrown in. I definitely felt more like a winner this time!

Good news though if you're cringing as you're reading this because you're back with my 1998 mentality. If you don't like negotiating, that's what your realtor is for. In fact, a recent report from the National Association of Realtors showed that 87 percent of buyers indicated that a top deciding factor for choosing a realtor is their negotiation skills.

A good real estate agent will be honest with you from the beginning, even with things you don't want to hear -- from the listing price to the negotiations. It's important to share what your priorities are and what your bottom line so that you have the negotiating power to win every time.

About Michael Gould, Realtor

Michael Gould is a real estate agent for Re/Max Eclipse in Waterford, Michigan. As a result of working with him, buyers and sellers find the home of their dreams, experience a smooth process, and do it all with ease, as quickly as possible.

Michael takes the stress out of buying and selling your home. He is committed to honestly and integrity in everything that he does.

Michael's mission is to create the most enjoyable buying and selling experience for his clients. He has been a real estate investor, prior stock broker and Corporate Commercial Credit Manager, Commercial Credit Manager, and Corporate Leasing Administrator.

On his off time, Michael enjoys fishing and hunting with his kids, working around the yard, gardening and driving his wife nuts.

Contact him at: mgould@remax.net

Facebook @michaelgouldrealtor
Linkedin @ michaelgouldrealtor